The faithful love of the LORD never ends! His mercies never cease. Great is his faithfulness; his mercies begin afresh each morning.

LAMENTATIONS 3:22-23 NLT

"Hope, in the biblical sense, means certainty and assurance. It is the firm, unshakable, indomitable belief that we will be raised from the dead (as Jesus was) and will be welcomed into our eternal home. That's enough to put joy in our heart and a spring in our step this day!"

—DAVID ROPER, *OUR DAILY BREAD*

O Lord, you alone are my hope.

PSALM 71:5 NLT

_____

_____

_____

_____

_____

_____

_____

_____

_____

_____

_____

_____

God asks us to loosen our grip on life, and in the process, our hearts will open to something new. He invites us to bring our expectations before Him with an attitude of hope, presenting our requests while trusting Him with the outcome. We put our hope not in the end result, but in God. He is the only One who will provide what we need, when we need it.

EXCERPTED FROM *MAKING PEACE WITH CHANGE*
BY GINA BRENNA BUTZ

No one is hopeless whose hope is in God.

_____
_____
_____
_____
_____
_____
_____
_____
_____
_____
_____
_____
_____
_____
_____
_____
_____
_____
_____
_____
_____
_____
_____

I wait for the LORD, my soul waits, and in his word I hope.

PSALM 130:5 ESV

Guide me in your truth and teach me,
for you are God my Savior, and
my hope is in you all day long.

PSALM 25:5 NIV

_____

_____

_____

_____

_____

_____

_____

_____

_____

_____

_____

_____

_____

_____

_____

_____

_____

_____

_____

_____

_____

_____

_____

_____

_____

_____

_____

_____

_____

_____

_____

_____

_____

_____

_____

_____

May the God of hope fill you with all joy and peace as you trust in him,
so that you may overflow with hope by the power of the Holy Spirit.

ROMANS 15:13 NIV

My hope is built on nothing less
Than Jesus' blood and righteousness;
I dare not trust the sweetest frame,
But wholly lean on Jesus' name.

> *On Christ, the solid Rock, I stand.*
> *All other ground is sinking sand;*
> *All other ground is sinking sand.*

When darkness seems to hide His face,
I rest on His unchanging grace.
In every high and stormy gale,
My anchor holds within the veil.

His oath, His covenant, His blood
Support me in the whelming flood;
When all around my soul gives way,
He then is all my hope and stay.

I long to stand like that. Firm. Unshakable. Steady. Fearless. Yes, I want that. But it's easy to get windblown in life's unexpected gales, and I often find myself teetering. I'm so grateful Jesus offers the strength and stability we could never find on our own. I want to intentionally proclaim, *On Christ, the solid Rock, I stand.* I want this to be my anthem when I'm succeeding and failing, climbing or falling, going toward something or away from it. I want a solid stance on the foundation I can trust, which will never ever crumble or let me down.

EXCERPTED FROM *HOW SWEET THE SOUND* BY LAURA L. SMITH

Preparing your minds for action, and being sober-minded,
set your hope fully on the grace that will be brought to you
at the revelation of Jesus Christ.

1 PETER 1:13 ESV

What circumstance or situation tempts you to give up hope? Surrender it to God today. Ask Him to give you promises to cling to and fill your heart with hope. (from *Refresh Your Faith* by Lori Hatcher)

GOD'S PROMISES I CLING TO:

-

-

-

-

-

-

Our faith becomes hope as we boldly depend on God.

Let us go right into the presence of God
with sincere hearts fully trusting him.

HEBREWS 10:22 NLT

The Bible promises that those who believe in Christ will have a Companion on the journey to help, encourage, and strengthen them in whatever may come their way. He is the One who has promised: "'I will never desert you, nor will I ever forsake you,' so that we confidently say, 'The Lord is my helper, I will not be afraid. What will man do to me?'" (Hebrews 13:5–6 NASB).

He is our sanctuary. To be able to have this confidence is to live a life that is an exclamation point in a world of question marks.

EXCERPTED FROM *MY HOPE IS IN YOU* BY BILL CROWDER

Faith and love ... spring from the hope stored up for you in heaven. ...
The gospel is bearing fruit and growing throughout the whole world.

COLOSSIANS 1:5-6 NIV

"The love of God gives us security, and the patience of Christ gives us consistency. We Christians should be the same day in and day out. We should refuse to become upset and thrown off by the circumstances so that we respond like the world around us. Stand firm! And hold to His teachings."

—RAY C. STEDMAN, *HOPE IN A CHAOTIC WORLD*

Continue in your faith, established and firm, and do not move from the hope held out in the gospel.

COLOSSIANS 1:23 NIV

_____

_____

_____

_____

_____

_____

_____

_____

_____

_____

_____

_____

_____

_____

Hope lies ahead. And that is because the Good Shepherd whose "goodness and love will follow" us "all the days" of our lives (Psalm 23:6) overtakes us in unexpected places. God's redeeming love is so indefatigable that He is able to take something the enemy has twisted and bend it back to a blessing. Roads that we wish we had never gone down can come out in places that are breathtakingly beautiful, precisely because of where we have been—and we could not have gotten there any other way.

EXCERPTED FROM *HOPE LIES AHEAD* BY JAMES BANKS

Brothers and sisters, we do not want you to be uninformed about those who sleep in death, so that you do not grieve like the rest of mankind, who have no hope. For we believe that Jesus died and rose again, and so we believe that God will bring with Jesus those who have fallen asleep in him.

1 THESSALONIANS 4:13-14 NIV

Blessed be the God and Father of our Lord Jesus Christ! According
to his great mercy, he has caused us to be born again to a living hope
through the resurrection of Jesus Christ from the dead, to an inheritance
that is imperishable, undefiled, and unfading, kept in heaven for you.

1 PETER 1:3-4 ESV

_____

_____

_____

_____

_____

_____

_____

_____

_____

_____

"Think about your family members who don't yet have a relationship with Christ. Pray and ask God to show you specific ways you can demonstrate love toward them. Ask Him to give you natural opportunities to share your faith. Then be brave and share your hope with them." (from *Refresh Your Faith* by Lori Hatcher)

I'M PRAYING FOR . . .

-

-

-

-

It is in this powerful name—the name of Jesus—that we sacrifice, follow, and cling. When we focus on Him and what He's done for us, our hearts are encouraged to deny self and live for Him. Nothing in this world compares to the hope we have in Christ.

And I am certain that God, who began the good work within you,
will continue his work until it is finally finished on the day
when Christ Jesus returns.

PHILIPPIANS 1:6 NLT

"Biblical hope is unique; it's a confident trust in God and what He is doing in the world and in our lives. That's something everyone needs! The writer of Hebrews clearly stated the importance of hope when he said, "Let us hold unswervingly to the hope we profess, for he who promised is faithful" (10:23 NIV). We hold fast to the hope we have received in Christ because our God is faithful."

—BILL CROWDER, *A DEEP DEPENDENCE*

Be of good courage, and He shall strengthen your heart,
all you who hope in the LORD.

PSALM 31:24 NKJV

_____

_____

_____

_____

_____

_____

_____

_____

_____

_____

For much of the world, hope is nothing more than a wish. "I hope I get that promotion," or "I hope things will get better." It has no foundation or object. When the winds of circumstance change, hope goes with it.

For believers, hope is so much more. It's inexorably linked to our trust in God. Several Hebrew words for trust may even be translated "to hope" in English. Jeremiah used one of these words when he said to God, "Our hope is in you" (Jeremiah 14:22). . . .

Christians, then, don't cling to a wispy thread of wishes. Instead, we base our hope for the future on God's faithfulness in the past. We stake our trust on God's character and faithfulness.

The psalmist who penned Psalm 27 articulated this thought when he said, "I would have lost heart, unless I had believed that I would see the goodness of the LORD in the land of the living" (v. 13 NKJV).

EXCERPTED FROM *REFRESH YOUR FAITH* BY LORI HATCHER

We rejoice in hope of the glory of God. Not only that, but we rejoice
in our sufferings, knowing that suffering produces endurance,
and endurance produces character, and character produces hope,
and hope does not put us to shame, because God's love has been
poured into our hearts through the Holy Spirit who has been given to us.

ROMANS 5:2-5 ESV

Hope is meant to overcome our greatest sorrow.

Weeping may endure for a night, but joy comes in the morning.

As for me, I look to the LORD for help.
I wait confidently for God to save me,
and my God will certainly hear me.

MICAH 7:7 NLT

God is the Hope-Giver who empowers us to persevere through the longest and darkest battles in life. God's children can declare what we know to be true, even in the middle of our pain-filled wait. We can sing about the Lord's proven faithfulness in Scripture, in the lives of others, and in our lives. We can join David and proclaim, "You, LORD, keep my lamp burning; my God turns my darkness into light" (Psalm 18:28 NIV).

EXCERPTED FROM *WAITING FOR GOD* BY XOCHITL DIXON

_____

_____

_____

_____

_____

_____

_____

_____

_____

_____

_____

_____

_____

_____

_____

_____

_____

_____

_____

_____

As the deer pants for streams of water, so my soul pants for you, my
God. . . . Why, my soul, are you downcast? Why so disturbed within me?
Put your hope in God, for I will yet praise him, my Savior and my God.

PSALM 42:1, 5 NIV

_____

_____

_____

_____

_____

_____

_____

_____

_____

_____

_____

_____

_____

_____

_____

_____

_____

_____

_____

"Hope is found not in the fact of the resurrection, but in the person of the Resurrected One. He is Lord of, and over, life and death."

—GARY INRIG, *THE MIRACLES*

May our Lord Jesus Christ himself and God our Father, who loved us
and by his grace gave us eternal encouragement and good hope,
encourage your hearts and strengthen you in every good deed and word.

2 THESSALONIANS 2:16-17 NIV

God offers hope when there is no hope. And hope is all one needs some-times—the assuring knowledge that God is there and that He cares. And from that hope our soul can emit praise to the One who is called Savior and God.

EXCERPTED FROM *BEYOND THE VALLEY* BY DAVE BRANON

Why am I discouraged? Why is my heart so sad? I will put my hope in God! I will praise him again—my Savior and my God!

PSALM 42:5-6 NLT

Let your steadfast love, O LORD, be upon us, even as we hope in you.

PSALM 33:22 ESV

SOURCES

Banks, James. *Hope Lies Ahead: Encouragement for Parents of Prodigals from a Family That's Been There*. Grand Rapids: MI: Our Daily Bread Publishing, 2020.

Branon, Dave. *Beyond the Valley: Finding Hope in Life's Losses*. Grand Rapids, MI: Our Daily Bread Publishing, 2020.

Butz, Gina Brenna. *Making Peace with Change: Navigating Life's Messy Transitions with Honesty and Grace*. Grand Rapids, MI: Our Daily Bread Publishing, 2020.

Crowder, Bill. *A Deep Dependence: 90 Our Daily Bread Reflections on Loving and Trusting God*. Grand Rapids, MI: Our Daily Bread Publishing, 2020.

———. *My Hope Is in You: Psalms that Comfort and Mend the Soul*. Grand Rapids, MI: Our Daily Bread Publishing, 2018.

Dixon, Xochitl. *Waiting for God: Trusting Daily in God's Plan and Pace*. Grand Rapids, MI: Our Daily Bread Publishing, 2019.

Hatcher, Lori. *Refresh Your Faith: Uncommon Devotions from Every Book of the Bible*. Grand Rapids, MI: Our Daily Bread Publishing, 2020.

Inrig, Gary. *The Miracles: Understanding What Jesus Did*. Grand Rapids, MI: Our Daily Bread Publishing, 2021.

Roper, David. *Our Daily Bread*, February 22, 2010.

Smith, Laura L. *How Sweet the Sound: The Power and Promise of 30 Beloved Hymns*. Grand Rapids, MI: Our Daily Bread Publishing, 2020.

Stedman, Ray C. *Hope in a Chaotic World: First and Second Thessalonians*. Grand Rapids, MI: Our Daily Bread Publishing, 1990, 2016.

Tate, Kim Cash. *Cling: Choosing a Lifestyle of Intimacy with God*. Grand Rapids, MI: Our Daily Bread Publishing, 2017.

PERMISSIONS AND CREDITS

For more resources from Our Daily Bread Publishing, visit odb.org/store.